Guide to

Practical Guide

A. De Quattro

Practical Guide

1.Introduction

Flask is a micro-framework for Python that enables the creation of lightweight and scalable web applications. It is appreciated for its simplicity and flexibility, allowing developers to choose the extensions and libraries they wish to integrate. This guide will provide a detailed overview of installing Flask, with a particular focus on system requirements, installation via `pip`, and configuring a virtual environment for an isolated development environment.

1.1 System Requirements

Before proceeding with the installation of Flask, it is important to ensure that the system meets all necessary requirements. Flask is compatible with most modern operating systems, but it is essential to have an appropriate version of Python and other supporting tools.

- **Supported Operating Systems:**

  - **Windows:** Flask works perfectly on all versions of Windows from Windows 7 onwards. However, it is recommended to use Windows 10 or later for better compatibility and performance.

  - **macOS:** All modern versions of macOS are compatible with Flask. However, macOS 10.13 (High Sierra) or later are recommended to fully utilize Python 3 features.

  - **Linux:** Flask is compatible with all major Linux distributions, such as Ubuntu, Fedora, CentOS, Debian, and others. It is essential to have Python 3.6 or later installed.

- **Python Version:** Flask requires Python 3.6 or later. Python 2.x is no longer supported by Flask, and using Python 2.x may lead to compatibility issues. To check the installed Python version, use the following command in the terminal:


```bash
```

```
python --version
```

or

```bash
python3 --version
```

The output should show the installed Python version. If the version is lower than 3.6, you will need to update Python.

- **Required Packages and Libraries:** In addition to Python, some packages and libraries might be necessary depending on the Flask extensions you want to use. However, for a simple Flask installation, no external dependencies are required.

2. Installation via pip

`pip` is the Python package manager and is the primary tool for installing Flask. If Python is installed correctly, `pip` should already be available. This section will explain how to install Flask using `pip`.

2.1 Checking pip

Before proceeding with the installation, you need to verify that `pip` is installed and correctly configured. This can be done by running the following command:

```bash
pip --version
```

or

```bash

pip3 --version

```

The output should show the installed `pip` version. If `pip` is not installed or not recognized, you will need to install it. On Linux distributions, `pip` can be installed with the following command:

```bash

sudo apt-get install python3-pip

```

On macOS, you can use `brew` (Homebrew) to install `pip`:

```bash

brew install python
```

```
```

On Windows, `pip` is installed automatically with Python. If needed, you can reinstall Python and ensure the option to install `pip` is selected during the installation process.

2.2 Installing Flask

Once `pip` is verified to be available, you can proceed with installing Flask. Here's how:

```bash
pip install Flask
```

This command will download and install the latest version of Flask and all its dependencies. During the installation process, `pip` may also automatically install other necessary packages for Flask, such as `Jinja2` for template rendering and `Werkzeug` for handling HTTP requests.

2.3 Verifying the Installation

After installing Flask, it is advisable to verify that the installation was successful. This can be done by creating a simple Python script that imports Flask and starts a test web server. Create a file named `app.py`:

```python
from flask import Flask

app = Flask(__name__)

@app.route('/')
def hello_world():
    return 'Hello, World!'
```

```
if __name__ == '__main__':

    app.run()
```

Run the file with the following command:

```bash
python app.py
```

If everything is configured correctly, you will see a message in the terminal indicating that the Flask server is running, and you can visit `http://127.0.0.1:5000/` in your browser to see the message "Hello, World!".

3. Configuring the Virtual Environment

When developing with Flask, it is good practice to use a virtual environment. A virtual environment is an isolated environment in which you can install Python packages specific to a project without affecting the operating system or other projects.

3.1 Creating the Virtual Environment

Python provides a module called `venv` for creating virtual environments. To create a virtual environment, run the following commands:

1. **Navigate to the project directory:**

Move to the directory where you want to create the virtual environment:

```bash
cd /path/to/project
```

2. **Create the virtual environment:**

Create a virtual environment named `venv`:

```bash
python3 -m venv venv
```

This command creates a new directory called `venv` that contains an isolated copy of the Python interpreter and a package environment.

3.2 Activating the Virtual Environment

To use the virtual environment, you need to activate it. The method to activate the virtual environment varies by operating system.

- **Windows:**

```bash
venv\Scripts\activate
```

- **macOS and Linux:**

```bash
source venv/bin/activate
```

After activating the virtual environment, the shell prompt will show the name of the environment (e.g., `(venv)`) at the beginning, indicating that the environment is active.

3.3 Installing Flask in the Virtual Environment

With the virtual environment active, you can install Flask within it using `pip`:

```bash
pip install Flask
```

This ensures that Flask and all its dependencies are installed only within the virtual environment, without affecting the global system or other projects.

3.4 Deactivating the Virtual Environment

After finishing work on the project, you can deactivate the virtual environment to return to the global Python interpreter. To deactivate the virtual environment, run:

```bash
```

```
deactivate

```
```
```

The shell prompt will return to normal, indicating that the virtual environment has been deactivated.

3.5 Benefits of Using Virtual Environments

Using virtual environments has several benefits:

- **Isolation:** Each project has its own environment, avoiding conflicts between package versions.

- **Portability:** You can share the virtual environment with other developers, ensuring that everyone uses the same configuration.

- **Cleanliness:** Keeps the global system clean, reducing the risk of compatibility issues between different projects.

4. Advanced Flask Configuration

In addition to basic configuration, there are several advanced options that can be useful during development with Flask. These include managing environment variables, configuring configuration files, and using Flask extensions.

4.1 Environment Variables

Flask can be configured using environment variables to manage settings such as the execution mode (development or production) and debugging configuration.

- **FLASK_APP:** Specifies the main file of the Flask application. For example:

```bash
export FLASK_APP=app.py
```

On Windows:

```bash
set FLASK_APP=app.py
```

- **FLASK_ENV:** Sets the execution environment. It can be set to `development` to enable debugging or `production` for production mode.

```bash
export FLASK_ENV=development
```

On Windows:

```bash
set FLASK_ENV=development
```

4.2 Configuration Files

Flask allows using configuration files to manage more complex settings. These files are usually written in Python and can be loaded into the Flask application.

For example, create a `config.py` file:

```python
class Config:
    DEBUG = True
    SECRET_KEY = 'supersecretkey'
```

```
```

Within the Flask application, load the configuration:

```python
app.config.from_object('config.Config')
```

4.3 Flask Extensions

Flask is highly modular and allows integration of extensions to add additional functionality such as database management, authentication, and more. Some popular extensions include:

- **Flask-SQLAlchemy:** For integration with SQL databases.

- **Flask-Migrate:** For managing database migrations.

- **Flask-Login:** For managing user authentication.

Extensions can be installed using `pip`:

```bash
pip install Flask-SQLAlchemy

pip install Flask-Migrate

pip install Flask-Login
```

After installation, extensions can be easily integrated into the Flask application.

5. Complete Example: Creating a Simple Flask Application

Now that we have covered the fundamental concepts, let's see how to create a simple Flask application using a virtual environment and custom configuration.

5.1 Project Setup

1. **Create the project structure:**

    ```bash
    mkdir my_flask_app
    cd my_flask_app
    ```

2. **Create the virtual environment and activate it:**

    ```bash
    python3 -m venv venv
    source venv/bin/activate
    ```

3. **Install Flask:**

```bash
pip install Flask
```

5.2 Creating the Flask Application

1. **Create the `app.py` file:**

```python
from flask import Flask, render_template

app = Flask(__name__)

@app.route('/')
def home():
```

```
    return 'Hello,

Flask!'

    if __name__ == '__main__':
        app.run(debug=True)
```

2. **Set the environment variables:**

```bash
export FLASK_APP=app.py
export FLASK_ENV=development
```

On Windows:

```bash
```

```
set FLASK_APP=app.py

set FLASK_ENV=development
```

3. **Run the application:**

```bash
flask run
```

Visit `http://127.0.0.1:5000/` in the browser to see the result.

5.3 Adding a Page with a Template

1. **Create a `templates` directory and an `index.html` file:**

```html
```

```
<!DOCTYPE html>
<html lang="en">
<head>
    <meta charset="UTF-8">
    <meta name="viewport" content="width=device-width, initial-scale=1.0">
    <title>My Flask App</title>
</head>
<body>
    <h1>{{ title }}</h1>
    <p>Welcome to {{ name }}!</p>
</body>
</html>
```

2. **Modify `app.py` to use the template:**

```python
```

```python
from flask import Flask, render_template

app = Flask(__name__)

@app.route('/')
def home():
    return render_template('index.html',
title='Home Page', name='Flask')

if __name__ == '__main__':
    app.run(debug=True)
```


3. **Reload the application and visit the homepage:**

The browser will now display the HTML template content, demonstrating how Flask can handle dynamic templates.

Flask is a flexible framework that allows developers to create web applications simply and modularly. With this guide, you have learned to install Flask, configure a virtual environment, and start developing a basic Flask application. By delving further into extensions and advanced configurations, you will be able to create robust and scalable web applications.

2.Basic Flask Concepts

Flask is a micro-framework for Python, widely used for developing lightweight and scalable web applications. Its popularity stems from its simplicity, flexibility, and minimalist approach, allowing developers to add only what they need without the burden of a heavy framework. This document provides an in-depth overview of the basic concepts of Flask, focusing on:

1. Creating a Flask app.

2. The structure of a Flask app.

3. Routing in Flask.

1. Creating a Flask App

1.1 Installing Flask

Before starting to create a Flask app, you need to install Flask on your system. As described in a previous section, Flask can be easily installed using `pip`, Python's package manager. It is recommended to work within a virtual environment to keep dependencies isolated. Here are the steps to create a virtual environment and install Flask:

1. **Creating the virtual environment:**

   ```bash
   python3 -m venv myenv
   ```

2. **Activating the virtual environment:**

   - On macOS/Linux:

   ```bash
   source myenv/bin/activate
   ```

- On Windows:

```bash
myenv\Scripts\activate
```

3. **Installing Flask:**

```bash
pip install Flask
```

1.2 Creating a Simple Flask App

Once Flask is installed, you can proceed to create your first application. The basic structure of a Flask app is very simple. Let's look at a minimal example:

1. **Creating the `app.py` file:**

Start by creating a file named `app.py` that will contain your application code.

```python
from flask import Flask

app = Flask(__name__)

@app.route('/')
def hello_world():
    return 'Hello, World!'

if __name__ == '__main__':
    app.run(debug=True)
```

2. **Running the app:**

To run the application, use the following command in the terminal:

```bash
python app.py
```

After running the command, you will see a message indicating that the Flask server is running. You can visit `http://127.0.0.1:5000/` in your browser to see your first working Flask app.

1.3 Code Explanation

- **Importing Flask:**

```python
```

```
from flask import Flask
```

The first line of the code imports the Flask module, necessary for accessing Flask's functionalities.

- **Creating the application:**

```python
app = Flask(__name__)
```

This line creates an instance of the Flask application. The variable name `app` is a common convention, but you can name it whatever you like. The `__name__` argument is passed to the Flask constructor to indicate the name of the current module, which helps Flask locate resources like templates and static files.

- **Defining a route:**

```python
@app.route('/')
def hello_world():
    return 'Hello, World!'
```

This is a route definition, which tells Flask which function to call when a user visits a particular URL. In this case, the `hello_world()` function is called when a user visits the homepage (`/`). The text `Hello, World!` is returned as an HTTP response to the browser.

- **Running the application:**

```python
```

```
if __name__ == '__main__':

    app.run(debug=True)

```

This condition ensures that the app runs only if the `app.py` file is executed directly and not imported as a module. The `debug=True` option enables debug mode, which provides detailed debugging information in case of errors and automatically reloads the server when code changes are made.

2. The Structure of a Flask App

As a Flask app grows in complexity, it's useful to organize the code in a structured way. In this section, we'll see how to organize a Flask app in a modular structure that makes it easier to manage the project as it evolves.

2.1 Basic Structure

The basic structure of a Flask app can be represented as follows:

```
```

my_flask_app/
│
├── app/
│   ├── __init__.py
│   ├── routes.py
│   ├── models.py
│   ├── templates/
│   │   └── base.html
│   └── static/
│   └── style.css
│
├── venv/
├── config.py
├── run.py
```
```

```
└── requirements.txt
```
```

- **my_flask_app/**: The main project directory.

- **app/**: The directory containing the Flask application.

- **`__init__.py`**: The file that initializes the Flask app.

- **routes.py**: File where the application's routes are defined.

- **models.py**: File where database models are defined.

- **templates/**: Directory for HTML templates.

- **static/**: Directory for static files like CSS, JavaScript, and images.

- **venv/**: The Python virtual environment.

- **config.py**: File for application configuration.

- **run.py**: The file to run the application.
```

- **requirements.txt**: File listing the project's Python dependencies.

2.2 Creating a Modularized Structure

Let's take a closer look at each component of the structure.

1. **`__init__.py`**

This file initializes the Flask app and can be used to configure the app settings, register blueprints, and attach extensions.

```python
from flask import Flask

def create_app():
    app = Flask(__name__)
```

```python
    # App configuration

    app.config.from_pyfile('config.py')


    # Register routes

    from .routes import main

    app.register_blueprint(main)


    return app
```

2. **routes.py**

This file contains all the route definitions for the application. Routes can be organized into blueprints to facilitate modularization.


```python
from flask import Blueprint,
```

render_template

```
main = Blueprint('main', __name__)

@main.route('/')
def home():
    return render_template('base.html')

@main.route('/about')
def about():
    return render_template('about.html')
```

In this example, we define a blueprint named `main`, which contains the routes for the homepage and the "about" page.

3. **models.py**

This file is where database models are defined if the app uses a relational database. Flask integrates well with SQLAlchemy, a popular Object-Relational Mapping (ORM) library.

```python
from flask_sqlalchemy import SQLAlchemy

db = SQLAlchemy()

class User(db.Model):
    id = db.Column(db.Integer, primary_key=True)
    username = db.Column(db.String(80), unique=True, nullable=False)
    email = db.Column(db.String(120), unique=True, nullable=False)

    def __repr__(self):
```

```
    return f'<User {self.username}>'
```
```
```

In this example, we define a `User` model with three fields: `id`, `username`, and `email`.

4. **templates/**

This directory contains HTML files that serve as templates for the application. Flask uses Jinja2 as its template engine, allowing you to insert Python logic within HTML files.

Example of a `base.html` file:

```html
<!DOCTYPE html>
<html lang="en">
<head>
```

```html
<meta charset="UTF-8">

<meta name="viewport" content="width=device-width, initial-scale=1.0">

<title>{% block title %}My Flask App{% endblock %}</title>

<link rel="stylesheet" href="{{ url_for('static', filename='style.css') }}">
  </head>
  <body>
    <header>
      <h1>Welcome to My Flask App</h1>
    </header>
    <div>
      {% block content %}{% endblock %}
    </div>
    <footer>
      <p>&copy; 2024 My Flask App</p>
    </footer>
```

```
</body>

</html>
```

This template defines a basic structure with `title` and `content` blocks that can be overridden in derived templates.

5. **static/**

The `static/` directory contains static files such as CSS, JavaScript, and images.

Example of a `style.css` file:

```css
body {
    font-family: Arial, sans-serif;
    background-color: #f4f4f4;
```

45

```css
    color: #333;

}


h1 {

    color: #007BFF;

}
```

6. **config.py**

This file contains the application's configurations, such as secret keys, database configurations, and other configuration variables.


```python
import os


class Config:
```

```
    SECRET_KEY =
os.environ.get('SECRET_KEY') or 'you-will-
never-guess'

    SQLALCHEMY_DATABASE_URI =
os.environ.get('DATABASE_URL') or \

        'sqlite:///my_flask_app.db'


SQLALCHEMY_TRACK_MODIFICATION
S = False

    ```
```

7. **run.py**

This file is used to run the application. You
can run the app directly from this file.


```python
from app import create_app


app = create_app()
```
```

```
if __name__ == '__main__':

    app.run()
```

8. **requirements.txt**

This file lists all the project dependencies, which can be installed using `pip`.

Example:

```
Flask==2.
```

1.2

```
Flask-SQLAlchemy==2.5.1
```

You can generate this file using the `pip freeze > requirements.txt` command.

Summary

Understanding the structure of a Flask app is crucial for building scalable and maintainable web applications. By organizing your app into modules, you can manage code efficiently, collaborate with team members, and easily extend your app's functionality. The modular approach also helps in isolating different parts of your app, making it easier to test and deploy.

3. Routing in Flask

Routing is a fundamental concept in Flask that allows you to map URLs to functions in your application. This section will cover the basics of routing in Flask, how to handle URL variables, and how to use HTTP methods within routes.

3.1 Basic Routing

In Flask, routing is defined using the `@app.route` decorator. Each route corresponds to a function in your application that handles the request to that URL. Here's an example:

```python
from flask import Flask

app = Flask(__name__)

@app.route('/')
def home():
    return 'This is the home page'
```

```
@app.route('/about')

def about():

    return 'This is the about page'


if __name__ == '__main__':

    app.run(debug=True)
```
```

In this example:


- The `/` URL is routed to the `home()` function.

- The `/about` URL is routed to the `about()` function.


#### 3.2 Routing with URL Variables


Flask allows you to pass variables in the URL, which can be accessed in the corresponding
```

view function. This is useful for creating dynamic URLs. Here's an example:

```python
@app.route('/user/<username>')
def show_user_profile(username):
    return f'User: {username}'
```

In this route, `<username>` is a variable part of the URL, which Flask passes to the `show_user_profile()` function as an argument. If you visit `/user/johndoe`, the function will return `User: johndoe`.

3.3 URL Variable Types

By default, Flask treats all URL variables as strings. However, you can specify different variable types like integers, floats, or paths. Here's how you can do it:

```python
@app.route('/post/<int:post_id>')
def show_post(post_id):
    return f'Post {post_id}'

@app.route('/path/<path:subpath>')
def show_subpath(subpath):
    return f'Subpath: {subpath}'
```

- `<int:post_id>` ensures that `post_id` is an integer.
- `<path:subpath>` captures the entire sub-path after `/path/`.

3.4 Using HTTP Methods

By default, Flask routes respond to GET requests. However, you can handle different

HTTP methods (GET, POST, PUT, DELETE, etc.) by specifying them in the route decorator.

Here's an example:

```python
@app.route('/submit', methods=['GET', 'POST'])
def submit_form():
    if request.method == 'POST':
        return 'Form Submitted'
    else:
        return 'Please Submit the Form'
```

In this route, the `submit_form()` function handles both GET and POST requests. Depending on the request method, it returns a different response.

Summary

Routing is a powerful feature in Flask that allows you to define the URLs of your web application and map them to specific functions. Understanding how to create routes, handle URL variables, and work with different HTTP methods is essential for building dynamic and interactive web applications with Flask.

This document provided a comprehensive overview of the basic concepts in Flask, covering how to create a Flask app, structure it for scalability, and handle routing. With this foundation, you can begin developing more complex applications, integrating databases, handling forms, and eventually deploying your Flask application to production.

In subsequent sections, you'll explore more advanced topics such as database integration, user authentication, and deploying your Flask app to a cloud platform.

3. Templates and Jinja2 in Flask

Flask is a micro-framework for web development in Python, and one of its key components is the template system. Templates allow for the separation of application logic from presentation, enabling developers to maintain cleaner and more modular code. In Flask, the default template engine is Jinja2, which provides powerful features for generating dynamic HTML.

This guide will explore Flask templates in detail, providing an introduction to basic concepts, an in-depth look at Jinja2, and an overview of filters and macros.

1. Introduction to Templates

1.1 What is a Template?

A template is a file that contains HTML

markup (or other types of markup) with placeholders or directives that can be replaced or executed with dynamic data. Templates are used to dynamically generate content, such as web pages, that can change based on the data provided by the server.

1.2 Benefits of Using Templates

Using templates in a web application offers several advantages:

- **Separation of Logic and Presentation:** Templates allow you to keep Python code separate from HTML code, making the application easier to maintain and develop.

- **Code Reusability:** With templates, you can define common page structures and reuse them in multiple parts of the application.

- **Ease of Updates:** Changes in presentation can be made within templates without modifying the application's logic.

- **Improved Collaboration:** Designers can

work on HTML templates while developers focus on backend logic, without interference.

1.3 The Jinja2 Template Engine

Jinja2 is the default template engine used by Flask. It was designed to be powerful and flexible, allowing developers to incorporate control logic within templates, such as loops, conditions, and filters.

Key Features of Jinja2:

- **Template Directives:** Such as `{% for %}`, `{% if %}`, and others, for controlling the flow of logic.

- **Variable Expressions:** Like `{{ variable }}` to dynamically insert data.

- **Filters:** Functions that can be applied to variables within templates to modify their output.

- **Macros:** Functions defined within templates for code reuse.

- **Blocks and Inheritance:** Mechanisms that allow the creation of flexible and reusable template structures.

1.4 Creating the First Template

To start using templates in Flask, let's create a simple Flask project and set up the first template.

1. **Create a Flask Project:**

   Create a directory for the project and a virtual environment:

   ```bash
   mkdir flask_template_project
   cd flask_template_project
   ```

```
python3 -m venv venv
source venv/bin/activate
```

Install Flask using pip:

```bash
pip install Flask
```

2. **Set Up the Basic Project Structure:**

Organize the project structure for easy management:

```
flask_template_project/
├── app/
```

```
|   ├── __init__.py
|   ├── templates/
|   |   └── index.html
|   └── routes.py
├── venv/
├── config.py
└── run.py
```

3. **Create the Flask App:**

In `app/__init__.py`, initialize the Flask application:

```python
from flask import Flask

def create_app():
```

```python
    app = Flask(__name__)

    from .routes import main
    app.register_blueprint(main)

    return app
```

In `app/routes.py`, define a simple route for the homepage:

```python
from flask import Blueprint, render_template

main = Blueprint('main', __name__)

@main.route('/')
def index():
```

```
    return render_template('index.html')
```

4. **Create the HTML Template:**

In `app/templates/index.html`, create a simple HTML file:

```html
<!DOCTYPE html>
<html lang="en">
<head>
    <meta charset="UTF-8">
    <meta name="viewport" content="width=device-width, initial-scale=1.0">
    <title>Home</title>
</head>
<body>
```

```
<h1>Welcome to My Flask App</h1>
<p>This is the homepage.</p>
</body>
</html>
```

5. **Run the App:**

Create `run.py` to run the app:

```python
from app import create_app

app = create_app()

if __name__ == '__main__':
    app.run(debug=True)
```

Start the app:

```bash
python run.py
```

Visit `http://127.0.0.1:5000/` in your browser to see the result.

2. Using Jinja2

Jinja2 offers a range of features that allow you to efficiently and flexibly manage logic within templates. In this section, we will explore how to use variables, loops, conditions, and template inheritance with Jinja2.

2.1 Inserting Variables into Templates

In Flask, you can pass variables from view functions to templates, which can then be displayed using Jinja2 variable expressions.

1. **Modify the Route to Pass a Variable:**

Update `routes.py` to pass a variable to the template:

```python
@main.route('/')
def index():
    user = "John Doe"
    return render_template('index.html', user=user)
```

2. **Use the Variable in the Template:**

Update `index.html` to display the user's name:

```html
<!DOCTYPE html>
<html lang="en">
<head>
    <meta charset="UTF-8">
    <meta name="viewport" content="width=device-width, initial-scale=1.0">
    <title>Home</title>
</head>
<body>
    <h1>Welcome to My Flask App</h1>
    <p>Hello, {{ user }}! This is the homepage.</p>
</body>
</html>
```

```
```

When you visit the homepage, you will see "Hello, John Doe!".

2.2 Loops in Templates

Jinja2 supports loops, allowing you to iterate over lists or other iterable objects within a template.

1. **Pass a List of Objects:**

   Update `routes.py` to pass a list of objects:

   ```python
   @main.route('/')
   def index():
       user = "John Doe"
   ```

```
   posts = [

      {'author': 'Alice', 'content': 'Hello, this
is Alice!'},

      {'author': 'Bob', 'content': 'Hi, I am
Bob!'},

      {'author': 'Charlie', 'content': 'Hey, it\'s
Charlie!'}

   ]

   return render_template('index.html',
user=user, posts=posts)

   ```
```

2. **Iterate Over Objects in the Template:**

Update `index.html` to iterate over the `posts` list:

```html
<!DOCTYPE html>
<html lang="en">
```
```

```html
<head>
    <meta charset="UTF-8">
    <meta name="viewport" content="width=device-width, initial-scale=1.0">
    <title>Home</title>
</head>
<body>
    <h1>Welcome to My Flask App</h1>
    <p>Hello, {{ user }}! Here are your posts:</p>

    <ul>
        {% for post in posts %}
<li><strong>{{ post.author }}</strong>: {{ post.content }}</li>
        {% endfor %}
    </ul>
</body>
```

```
</html>
```

This code iterates over the `posts` list and displays each post with the author and content.

2.3 Conditions in Templates

Jinja2 also supports conditions, allowing you to execute conditional logic within templates.

1. **Add a Condition:**

Suppose you want to show a special message if the user has no posts.

Update `index.html` with a condition:

```html
```

```html
<!DOCTYPE html>
<html lang="en">
<head>
    <meta charset="UTF-8">
    <meta name="viewport" content="width=device-width, initial-scale=1.0">
    <title>Home</title>
</head>
<body>
    <h1>Welcome to My Flask App</h1>
    <p>Hello, {{ user }}!</p>

    {% if posts %}
        <ul>
            {% for post in posts %}
<li><strong>{{ post.author }}</strong>: {{ post.content }}</li>
```

```
    {% endfor %}
  </ul>
 {% else %}
   <p>You have no posts.</p>
 {% endif %}
</body>
</html>
```

If `posts` is empty, the message "You have no posts" will be displayed.

2.4 Template Inheritance

One of the most powerful concepts in Jinja2 is template inheritance, which allows you to create reusable and modular page structures.

1. **Create a Base Template:**

In `app/templates/`, create a `base.html` file:

```html
<!DOCTYPE html>
<html lang="en">
<head>
    <meta charset="UTF-8">
    <meta name="viewport" content="width=device-width, initial-scale=1.0">
    <title>{% block title %}My Flask App{% endblock %}</title>
</head>
<body>
    <header>
        <h1>My Flask App</h1>
    </header>
```

```html
<nav>
    <ul>
        <li><a href="/">Home</a></li>
        <li><a href="/about">About</a></li>
    </ul>
</nav>

<main>
    {% block content %} {% endblock %}
</main>

<footer>
    <p>&copy; 2024 My Flask App</p>
</footer>
```

```
</body>
</html>
```

2. **Extend the Base Template:**

Update `index.html` to extend `base.html`:

```html
{% extends 'base.html' %}

{% block title %}Home{% endblock %}

{% block content %}
<p>Hello, {{ user }}! Welcome to the homepage.</p>

{% if posts %}
```

```
<ul>
    {% for post in posts %}

<li><strong>{{ post.author }}</strong>: {{ post.content }}</li>
        {% endfor %}
    </ul>
  {% else %}
    <p>You have no posts.</p>
  {% endif %}
  {% endblock %}
```

By using `{% extends %}`, this template inherits the structure from `base.html` and only needs to define the content for specific blocks.

3. Filters and Macros in Jinja2

Jinja2 includes various built-in filters and allows you to define your own filters and macros to make template code more readable and reusable.

3.1 Using Filters

Filters are functions that modify the value of a variable in a template. For example:

1. **Uppercase Filter:**

    ```html
    <p>{{ user|upper }}</p>
    ```

    This will display the user's name in uppercase.

2. **Custom Filters:**

You can also define custom filters in Flask:

```python
from flask import Flask

app = Flask(__name__)

@app.template_filter('reverse')
def reverse_filter(s):
    return s[::-1]
```

Then use the custom filter in the template:

```html
<p>{{ user|reverse }}</p>
```

3.2 Defining Macros

Macros in Jinja2 are like functions in Python and can be used to encapsulate code for reuse.

1. **Create a Macro:**

    Define a macro in a separate file `app/templates/macros.html`:

    ```html
    {% macro render_post(post) %}
    <li><strong>{{ post.author }}</strong>: {{ post.content }}</li>
    {% endmacro %}
    ```

2. **Use the Macro in a Template:**

Import and use the macro in `index.html`:

```html
{% from 'macros.html' import render_post %}

{% block content %}
<p>Hello, {{ user }}! Welcome to the homepage.</p>

{% if posts %}
    <ul>
        {% for post in posts %}
            {{ render_post(post) }}
        {% endfor %}
    </ul>
{% else %}
    <p>You have no posts.</p>
```

```
{% endif %}

{% endblock %}
```

```
```

Macros are useful for avoiding repetition in templates and keeping the code clean and maintainable.

With these concepts in mind, you can create complex and dynamic web applications with Flask and Jinja2, taking full advantage of templates to manage the presentation layer efficiently.

4. Request Handling in Flask

Request handling is one of the fundamental aspects of developing web applications with Flask. Flask provides a set of tools that allow for efficient and flexible management of HTTP requests, extracting URL parameters, handling form data, and configuring communication with databases. In this document, we will explore the various aspects of request handling in Flask in detail.

1. Types of HTTP Requests

The HTTP protocol (HyperText Transfer Protocol) is the foundation of web communication. Every interaction between a client (such as a web browser) and a server occurs through HTTP requests. Flask can handle different types of HTTP requests, each with a specific meaning and purpose.

1.1 HTTP Methods

The most common HTTP methods used in Flask applications are:

- **GET**: Used to request data from a server. This is the default method for HTTP requests and does not modify data on the server. For example, when you visit a webpage, the browser sends a GET request to the server.

- **POST**: Used to send data to the server, often to create or update resources. It is commonly used in HTML forms, where form data is sent to the server for processing.

- **PUT**: Used to completely update an existing resource on the server with the provided data. Unlike POST, PUT is idempotent, meaning that repeated PUT requests with the same data will have the same effect.

- **PATCH**: Similar to PUT but used to

make partial changes to an existing resource.

- **DELETE**: Used to delete an existing resource on the server.

- **HEAD**: Similar to GET, but the server's response does not contain a body. It is used to obtain only the metadata of a resource.

- **OPTIONS**: Used to obtain the communication options supported by a server or a specific resource.

1.2 Examples of Using HTTP Methods in Flask

In Flask, different HTTP methods can be handled using view functions. Each route can be configured to respond to one or more HTTP methods.

1. **Handling GET Requests:**

A simple view function that responds to a GET request could be as follows:

```python
from flask import Flask, jsonify

app = Flask(__name__)

@app.route('/hello', methods=['GET'])
def hello():
    return jsonify(message="Hello, World!")
```

In this example, the `/hello` route only responds to GET requests and returns a JSON message.

2. **Handling POST Requests:**

Here's an example of handling a POST request:

```python
from flask import Flask, request, jsonify

app = Flask(__name__)

@app.route('/submit', methods=['POST'])
def submit():
    data = request.json
    name = data.get('name')
    return jsonify(message=f"Hello, {name}!")
```

In this case, the `/submit` route accepts

JSON data sent with a POST request, extracts the name, and returns a personalized message.

3. **Handling PUT and DELETE Requests:**

Flask can also handle PUT and DELETE requests just as easily:

```python
@app.route('/update/<int:item_id>',
methods=['PUT'])

def update_item(item_id):

    # Code to update the item with item_id

    return jsonify(message=f"Item {item_id}
updated.")


@app.route('/delete/<int:item_id>',
methods=['DELETE'])

def delete_item(item_id):

    # Code to delete the item with item_id
```

88

```
    return jsonify(message=f"Item {item_id}
deleted.")

    ```
```

Here, `update_item` and `delete_item`
handle PUT and DELETE requests for a
specific item identified by the `item_id`
parameter, respectively.

1.3 Differences Between GET and POST

One of the main distinctions between GET
and POST concerns how data is sent to the
server:

- **GET**: Data is included in the request
URL as query string parameters. This means
that the data is visible in the URL, which has
limitations in terms of length and security.

- **POST**: Data is sent in the body of the
```

request, allowing for larger amounts of data to be sent and making it less visible, thus improving security.

In general, GET is used to request information without side effects, while POST is used for actions that modify the server's state, such as submitting forms or creating new resources.

2. Using Request and Response Objects

Flask provides two central objects for handling HTTP requests and responses: `request` and `response`. These objects allow you to access the details of the HTTP request and to construct the response to be sent back to the client.

2.1 The Request Object

The `request` object in Flask represents the HTTP request sent from the client to the server. This object allows access to a wide range of information, such as form data, URL parameters, JSON data, uploaded files, and more.

1. **Accessing Query String Parameters:**

When a GET request contains parameters in the query string, they can be extracted using `request.args`.

```python
@app.route('/search', methods=['GET'])
def search():
    query = request.args.get('q')
    return jsonify(message=f"Search results for: {query}")
```

If the URL is `/search?q=flask`, the variable

`query` will contain the value `flask`.

2. **Accessing Form Data:**

When a POST request sends form data, it can be extracted using `request.form`.

```python
@app.route('/login', methods=['POST'])
def login():
    username = request.form['username']
    password = request.form['password']
    return jsonify(message=f"Logged in as: {username}")
```

In this case, `username` and `password` are extracted from the data sent by the form.

3. **Accessing JSON Data:**

Flask also simplifies access to JSON data sent in a POST request.

```python
@app.route('/api/data', methods=['POST'])
def get_json_data():
    data = request.json
    return jsonify(data)
```

Using `request.json`, the JSON data can be easily extracted and processed.

4. **Accessing Request Headers:**

HTTP headers can be accessed through `request.headers`.

```python
@app.route('/headers', methods=['GET'])

def headers():

    user_agent = request.headers.get('User-Agent')

    return jsonify(user_agent=user_agent)
```

This code returns the `User-Agent` header, which contains information about the client that sent the request.

5. **Handling Uploaded Files:**

Flask allows handling files uploaded by the client using `request.files`.

```python
```

```python
@app.route('/upload', methods=['POST'])
def upload_file():
    if 'file' not in request.files:
        return jsonify(message="No file part")
    file = request.files['file']
    if file.filename == ":
        return jsonify(message="No selected file")
    # Save the file
    file.save(f"/path/to/save/{file.filename}")
    return jsonify(message="File uploaded successfully")
```

This example shows how to handle a file uploaded by the client and save it on the server.

2.2 The Response Object

The `response` object in Flask represents the HTTP response sent from the server to the client. Flask provides several ways to create and manipulate a response.

1. **Creating a Simple Response:**

The simplest way to create a response is to return a string from a view function.

```python
@app.route('/simple')
def simple_response():
    return "This is a simple response"
```

This string will be used as the response body and sent to the client with a default HTTP 200 (OK) status code.

2. **Using `make_response`:**

Flask provides the `make_response` function to create a more complex response that can include custom headers and status codes.

```python
from flask import make_response

@app.route('/custom_response')

def custom_response():

    response = make_response("This is a custom response", 404)

    response.headers['Custom-Header'] = 'CustomValue'

    return response
```

In this example, the response has a 404

(Not Found) status code and includes a custom header.

3. **Using JSON in Responses:**

Flask also provides an easy way to return JSON data using `jsonify`.

```python
@app.route('/json_response')

def json_response():

    return jsonify(status="success", data={"key": "value"})
```

The `jsonify` function automatically converts a Python dictionary into a JSON object and sets the `Content-Type` header to `application/json`.

4. **Redirects:**

Flask supports redirects, which can be created using the `redirect` function.

```python
from flask import redirect, url_for

@app.route('/go-to-home')
def go_to_home():
    return redirect(url_for('home'))
```

This example redirects the user to the `home` function using `url_for` to generate the URL.

5. **Cookies in Responses:**

Cookies can be set using the `response` object.

```python
@app.route('/set-cookie')

def set_cookie():

    response = make_response("Setting a cookie")

    response.set_cookie('username', 'flask_user')

    return response
```

This code sets a `username` cookie with the value `flask_user`.

2.3 Manipulating Status Codes

In Flask, you can specify the HTTP status code of the response by returning a tuple containing the response body and the status code.

```python
@app.route('/not-found')

def not

_found():
    return "This resource was not found", 404
```

In this example, the response body is "This resource was not found," and the status code is 404 (Not Found).

3. Handling JSON Data in Flask

Handling JSON data is a common task in web applications, especially in RESTful APIs. Flask provides comprehensive support for working with JSON data, making it easy to send and receive JSON objects in HTTP requests and responses.

3.1 Receiving JSON Data in Requests

When a client sends JSON data in a POST request, Flask allows you to easily access it using `request.json`.

```python
@app.route('/process_json',
methods=['POST'])

def process_json():

    data = request.json

    key_value = data.get('key')

    return jsonify(received=key_value)
```

In this example, the JSON data sent in the

request body is accessed via `request.json`, and the value associated with the `key` is returned in the response.

3.2 Sending JSON Responses

Flask provides a simple and convenient way to send JSON responses using `jsonify`.

```python
@app.route('/json_output')

def json_output():

    return jsonify(status="success", data={"key": "value"})
```

The `jsonify` function automatically converts a Python dictionary into a JSON object and sets the appropriate `Content-Type` header.

3.3 Handling Errors in JSON Requests

When dealing with JSON data, it's essential to handle errors gracefully, such as when the client sends malformed JSON or fails to include required fields.

```python
from flask import abort

@app.route('/safe_process',
methods=['POST'])
def safe_process():
    if not request.is_json:
        abort(400, description="Invalid JSON format")
    data = request.json
    if 'key' not in data:
        abort(400, description="Missing 'key' in JSON data")
```

```
    return jsonify(status="success",
received=data['key'])

```

In this example, the view function checks if the request contains valid JSON data and whether the `key` is present. If not, a 400 (Bad Request) error is returned with a descriptive message.

Flask's request and response handling capabilities provide the flexibility needed for building robust web applications and APIs. By understanding the different types of HTTP requests, effectively using the `request` and `response` objects, and properly handling JSON data, developers can create secure and efficient web services that cater to various client needs.

5.Authentication, Authorization, and Error Handling in Flask

Flask is a powerful framework for developing web applications in Python. To build robust web applications, it is essential to implement authentication and authorization mechanisms, handle errors effectively, and thoroughly test the code. In this guide, we will explore in detail how to address each of these aspects using Flask and its extensions.

1. Authentication and Authorization

Authentication and authorization are two critical components for the security of web applications. Authentication verifies the identity of the user, while authorization determines whether a user has permission to access specific resources.

1.1 Introduction to Authentication

Authentication is the process of verifying a user's identity. This process can include various methods, such as:

- **Username and Password**: The most common method, where the user enters a username and password.

- **Token**: Used for APIs, where a token is passed with each request to authenticate the user.

- **OAuth**: A protocol for authorizing third-party access, such as logging in with Google or Facebook.

1.2 Using Flask-Login

Flask-Login is a Flask extension that simplifies user authentication and session management. It provides tools for handling login, logout, and checking the authentication status of the user.

1.2.1 Installing Flask-Login

To install Flask-Login, use pip:

```bash
pip install Flask-Login
```

1.2.2 Configuring Flask-Login

Start by importing and configuring Flask-Login in your Flask application.

```python
from flask import Flask, redirect, url_for, render_template

from flask_login import LoginManager, UserMixin, login_user, login_required, logout_user, current_user
```

```
app = Flask(__name__)

app.secret_key = 'supersecretkey'  # Necessary
for session protection


login_manager = LoginManager()

login_manager.init_app(app)

login_manager.login_view = 'login'

```
```

`login_manager.login_view` defines which
view to show if the user is not authenticated
and tries to access a protected view.

1.2.3 Creating a User Model

Define a user model that implements
`UserMixin`, provided by Flask-Login, to
obtain the necessary methods for
authentication.
```

```python
from flask_sqlalchemy import SQLAlchemy

db = SQLAlchemy(app)

class User(db.Model, UserMixin):
    id = db.Column(db.Integer, primary_key=True)

    username = db.Column(db.String(150), unique=True, nullable=False)

    password = db.Column(db.String(150), nullable=False)
```

1.2.4 Loading the User

Define a function to load a user from the session.

```python
@login_manager.user_loader
def load_user(user_id):
    return User.query.get(int(user_id))
```

1.2.5 Implementing Login and Logout

Add routes for login and logout, using `login_user` and `logout_user` provided by Flask-Login.

```python
from flask import request, flash

@app.route('/login', methods=['GET', 'POST'])
def login():
```

```python
    if request.method == 'POST':

        username = request.form['username']

        password = request.form['password']

        user =
User.query.filter_by(username=username).firs
t()

        if user and user.password == password:
# Plaintext password; use hashing in
production

            login_user(user)

            return redirect(url_for('profile'))

        else:

            flash('Invalid username or password')

    return render_template('login.html')


@app.route('/logout')

@login_required

def logout():

    logout_user()
```

```
    return redirect(url_for('login'))
```

In this example, `login_required` is a decorator that protects the routes, requiring the user to be authenticated.

1.2.6 Protecting Routes

To protect routes, use the `login_required` decorator.

```python
@app.route('/profile')

@login_required

def profile():

    return f"Welcome,
{current_user.username}!"
```

This route is accessible only to authenticated users, and `current_user` represents the currently authenticated user.

1.3 Authorization

Authorization deals with determining whether a user has permission to access specific resources. Flask-Login focuses on authentication, while authorization must be implemented separately.

1.3.1 Role-Based Authorization

To implement role-based authorization, add a `role` field to the `User` model.

```python
class User(db.Model, UserMixin):
    id = db.Column(db.Integer, primary_key=True)
```

```python
    username = db.Column(db.String(150),
unique=True, nullable=False)

    password = db.Column(db.String(150),
nullable=False)

    role = db.Column(db.String(50),
nullable=False)
```

Define custom decorators to protect routes based on roles.

```python
from functools import wraps

from flask import request, redirect, url_for


def admin_required(f):

    @wraps(f)

    def decorated_function(*args, **kwargs):

        if not current_user.is_authenticated or
current_user.role != 'admin':
```

```
    return redirect(url_for('login'))

    return f(*args, **kwargs)

  return decorated_function


@app.route('/admin')

@admin_required

def admin_dashboard():

    return "Admin Dashboard"

```

2. Error Handling

Managing errors in a web application is crucial for ensuring a good user experience and for facilitating problem resolution.

2.1 Error Handling

Flask provides various mechanisms for

handling errors, including using `try`/`except` blocks and registering custom error handlers.

2.1.1 Handling Errors with Try/Except

You can use `try`/`except` blocks to handle errors within your view functions.

```python
@app.route('/divide/<int:a>/<int:b>')
def divide(a, b):
    try:
        result = a / b
    except ZeroDivisionError:
        return "Cannot divide by zero", 400
    return f"Result is {result}"
```

2.1.2 Global Error Handling

To handle errors globally, use Flask's error handlers.

```python
@app.errorhandler(404)
def not_found_error(error):
    return render_template('404.html'), 404

@app.errorhandler(500)
def internal_error(error):
    return render_template('500.html'), 500
```

In this example, Flask renders custom error pages for 404 and 500 errors.

2.2 Creating Custom Error Pages

To provide a better user experience, you can create custom error pages.

2.2.1 Creating Error Templates

Create HTML templates for error pages, such as `404.html` and `500.html`.

404.html

```html
<!doctype html>
<html lang="en">
<head>
    <meta charset="utf-8">
    <title>Page Not Found</title>
</head>
<body>
    <h1>404 - Page Not Found</h1>
```

    <p>The page you are looking for does not exist.</p>

</body>

</html>

```


**500.html**


```html
<!doctype html>

<html lang="en">

<head>

   <meta charset="utf-8">

   <title>Internal Server Error</title>

</head>

<body>

   <h1>500 - Internal Server Error</h1>

   <p>There was an error processing your request.</p>

```
</body>
</html>
```

2.3 Error Logging

Use Python's `logging` module to log errors and warnings.

```python
import logging
from logging.handlers import RotatingFileHandler

if not app.debug:
    handler = RotatingFileHandler('error.log', maxBytes=10000, backupCount=1)
    handler.setLevel(logging.ERROR)
    app.logger.addHandler(handler)
```

```
```

This configuration creates a log file that records application errors.

3. Testing Flask Applications

Testing is a fundamental part of software development to ensure that the code works as expected and to detect any bugs before deployment.

3.1 Writing Unit Tests

Flask is compatible with Python's unit tests, which allow you to test individual functions and methods in isolation.

3.1.1 Setting Up the Test Environment

To test your application, you need to set up a separate test environment. Flask uses a test app that can be created as follows:

```python
import unittest

class FlaskTestCase(unittest.TestCase):
    def setUp(self):
        app.config['TESTING'] = True

app.config['SQLALCHEMY_DATABASE_URI'] = 'sqlite:///test.db'
        self.app = app.test_client()
        self.app_context = app.app_context()
        self.app_context.push()

    def tearDown(self):
        self.app_context.pop()
```

```
```

3.1.2 Writing Tests

Write unit tests for your view functions and other parts of the code.

```python
class FlaskTestCase(unittest.TestCase):

    def setUp(self):

        app.config['TESTING'] = True

        app.config['SQLALCHEMY_DATABASE_URI'] = 'sqlite:///test.db'

        self.app = app.test_client()

        self.app_context = app.app_context()

        self.app_context.push()


    def tearDown(self):
```

```python
        self.app_context.pop()


    def test_login(self):

        response = self.app.post('/login',
data=dict(username='test',
password='password'))

        self.assertEqual(response.status_code,
200)


    def test_profile_access(self):

        self.app.post('/login',
data=dict(username='test',
password='password'))

        response = self.app.get('/profile')

        self.assertEqual(response.status_code,
200)
```
```

### 3.2 Testing Routes
```

To test routes, use Flask's `test_client` object, which simulates HTTP requests.

```python
def test_home_page(self):

    response = self.app.get('/')

    self.assertEqual(response.status_code, 200

)

    self.assertIn(b'Welcome to the Home Page', response.data)
```

3.3 Using Flask-Testing

Flask-Testing is an extension that enhances Flask's testing capabilities by providing additional tools for testing Flask applications.

3.3.1 Installing Flask-Testing

Install Flask-Testing with pip:

```bash
pip install Flask-Testing
```

3.3.2 Using Flask-Testing

Incorporate Flask-Testing into your test class to use its additional features.

```python
from flask_testing import TestCase

class MyTestCase(TestCase):
    def create_app(self):
```

```
    app.config['TESTING'] = True

app.config['SQLALCHEMY_DATABASE_U
RI'] = 'sqlite:///test.db'

    return app


  def test_example(self):

    response = self.client.get('/')

    self.assert200(response)

    self.assert_template_used('index.html')
```
```

`Flask-Testing` provides useful methods such as `assert200` and `assert_template_used` to verify response status and template usage.

Handling authentication and authorization, managing errors, and testing applications are fundamental aspects of developing secure and reliable web applications with Flask. By using the Flask-Login and Flask-Testing extensions,
```

you can implement robust authentication solutions, manage errors effectively, and ensure the quality of your code through well-structured tests. By following best practices and using the right tools, you can build scalable and maintainable Flask applications.

6.Deployment of Flask App, Extensions, and Best Practices

Deploying a Flask application in production, utilizing extensions to expand its functionality, and adhering to best practices are crucial aspects to ensure the success and security of your web applications. This guide will explore in detail how to prepare a Flask app for production, different hosting methods, using Docker, Flask extensions, and best practices to optimize and secure your application.

1. Deploying the Flask App

Deploying a Flask app requires proper preparation to ensure that the app is secure, performant, and scalable. Deployment can occur on various servers and utilize technologies like Docker to simplify environment management.

1.1 Production Preparation

When preparing a Flask app for production, several aspects need to be considered:

1.1.1 Environment Configuration

- **Setting Production Mode:**

  Set the Flask environment to production mode to disable the debugger and enable optimizations.

  ```python
  app.config['ENV'] = 'production'
  app.config['DEBUG'] = False
  ```

- **Managing Secret Keys:**

  Ensure that the secret key used for signing

cookies and managing sessions is secure and unique.

```python
app.secret_key = 'your-secret-key'
```

In production, it's advisable to manage the secret key through an environment variable.

- **Logging Configuration:**

Set up logging to monitor and record important events and errors.

```python
import logging

from logging.handlers import RotatingFileHandler
```

```
if not app.debug:

    handler = RotatingFileHandler('app.log',
maxBytes=10000, backupCount=1)

    handler.setLevel(logging.INFO)

    app.logger.addHandler(handler)
```
```

#### 1.1.2 Performance Optimization

- **Caching:**

  Use caching to reduce server load and improve response times.

  - **Flask-Caching** is an extension that supports various caching backends, like Redis or Memcached.

- **Compression:**

  Enable HTTP response compression to reduce the size of transferred data.
```

- **Flask-Compress** is a useful extension for compressing HTTP responses.

- **Database Optimization:**

  Ensure queries are efficient and use appropriate indexes.

1.1.3 Security

- **Dependency Management:**

  Keep libraries and packages up to date to avoid known vulnerabilities.

- **Protection Against Common Attacks:**

  Implement security measures such as CSRF and XSS protection.

  - **Flask-WTF** offers CSRF protection support in forms.

- **HTTPS Configuration:**

  Use HTTPS to encrypt traffic between the client and the server. You can use services like Let's Encrypt to obtain free SSL certificates.

1.2 Hosting the App on Different Servers

Once the Flask app is prepared for production, you can host it on various types of servers. Here's an overview of the most common hosting methods:

1.2.1 Cloud Hosting Services

- **Heroku:**

  Heroku is a cloud platform that simplifies the deployment and management of web applications. You can deploy a Flask app on Heroku by following these steps:

- Create a `requirements.txt` file with all dependencies.

```bash
pip freeze > requirements.txt
```

- Create a `Procfile` to specify the app's startup command.

```
web: gunicorn app:app
```

- Initialize a Git repository, add files, and deploy to Heroku.

```bash
git init
```

```
git add .

git commit -m "Initial commit"

heroku create

git push heroku master
```

- **AWS Elastic Beanstalk:**

 AWS Elastic Beanstalk is a service that automatically manages provisioning, load balancing, and scaling. To deploy a Flask app:

 - Install the Elastic Beanstalk CLI.

 ```bash
 pip install awsebcli
 ```

 - Create a new application and environment.

```bash
eb init
eb create
```

- Deploy the app.

```bash
eb deploy
```

1.2.2 Virtual Servers and VPS

- **DigitalOcean, Linode, AWS EC2:**

These services offer virtual servers that you can manually configure to host your application. Here's an example setup on an Ubuntu server:

- Install dependencies.

```bash
sudo apt update

sudo apt install python3-pip python3-venv nginx
```

- Set up a virtual environment and install dependencies.

```bash
python3 -m venv venv

source venv/bin/activate

pip install flask gunicorn
```

- Configure Gunicorn as the WSGI server and Nginx as a reverse proxy.

- Create a service file for Gunicorn at `/etc/systemd/system/myapp.service`.

```ini
[Unit]

Description=gunicorn instance to serve myapp

After=network.target


[Service]

User=yourusername

Group=www-data

WorkingDirectory=/path/to/your/application

ExecStart=/path/to/your/venv/bin/gunicorn -w 4 -b 127.0.0.1:8000 app:app


[Install]

WantedBy=multi-user.target
```

```
```

- Configure Nginx at `/etc/nginx/sites-available/myapp`.

```nginx
server {
    listen 80;

    server_name yourdomain.com;

    location / {
        proxy_pass http://127.0.0.1:8000;

        proxy_set_header Host $host;

        proxy_set_header X-Real-IP $remote_addr;

        proxy_set_header X-Forwarded-For $proxy_add_x_forwarded_for;

        proxy_set_header X-Forwarded-Proto $scheme;
```

```
    }

  }

  ```
```

- Enable the site and restart Nginx.

```bash
sudo ln -s /etc/nginx/sites-available/myapp
/etc/nginx/sites-enabled

sudo systemctl restart nginx
```

1.3 Using Docker with Flask

Docker simplifies application deployment by isolating the runtime environment within containers.

1.3.1 Creating a Dockerfile
```

A `Dockerfile` defines the environment in which the Flask app will run.

```dockerfile
# Use a base Python image
FROM python:3.10-slim

# Set the working directory
WORKDIR /app

# Copy requirements file and install dependencies
COPY requirements.txt requirements.txt
RUN pip install -r requirements.txt

# Copy the rest of the app code
COPY . .

# Expose the port Flask listens on
```

```
EXPOSE 5000

# Command to start the app

CMD ["gunicorn", "-b", "0.0.0.0:5000",
"app:app"]
```

1.3.2 Creating a `docker-compose.yml` File

Docker Compose simplifies managing multiple containers.

```yaml
version: '3'
services:
  web:
    build: .
    ports:
```

        - "5000:5000"

```
```

1.3.3 Building and Starting Containers

- Build the Docker image.

  ```bash
  docker build -t myflaskapp .
  ```

- Start the containers with Docker Compose.

  ```bash
  docker-compose up
  ```

These steps create and start a Docker

container for your Flask application.

2. Flask Extensions

Flask extensions add extra functionality, simplifying integration with common services and tools.

2.1 Introduction to Extensions

Flask is designed to be simple and modular, allowing the use of extensions to add functionality without complicating the core framework. Extensions can handle various aspects, such as authentication, database management, and form validation.

2.2 Popular Extensions and Their Use

Here are some popular Flask extensions and how to use them:

2.2.1 Flask-SQLAlchemy

Flask-SQLAlchemy integrates SQLAlchemy with Flask, making database management easier.

- **Installation:**

  ```bash
  pip install Flask-SQLAlchemy
  ```

- **Configuration:**

  ```python
  from flask_sqlalchemy import SQLAlchemy

app.config['SQLALCHEMY_DATABASE_URI'] = 'sqlite:///mydatabase.db'
  ```

```python
db = SQLAlchemy(app)
```

- **Model Definition:**

```python
class User(db.Model):
    id = db.Column(db.Integer, primary_key=True)
    username = db.Column(db.String(150), unique=True, nullable=False)
    email = db.Column(db.String(150), unique=True, nullable=False)
```

2.2.2 Flask-WTF

Flask-WTF is an extension for working with forms in Flask, offering features like CSRF protection and form validation.

- **Installation:**

```bash
pip install Flask-WTF
```

- **Configuration:**

```python
from flask_wtf import FlaskForm
from wtforms import StringField, PasswordField
from wtforms.validators import InputRequired, Email


class LoginForm(FlaskForm):
    username = StringField('Username', validators=[InputRequired()])
```

```python
    password = PasswordField('Password',
validators=[InputRequired()])
```

Certainly! Continuing from where we left off:

2.2.3 Flask-Login (continued)

- **User and Login Definition:**

```python
from flask_login import UserMixin,
login_user

class User(UserMixin):
    # User model definition

@app.route('/login', methods=['POST'])
def login():
```

```
    user =
User.query.filter_by(username='user').first()

    if user:

        login_user(user)

        return redirect(url_for('profile'))
    ```
```

#### 2.2.4 Flask-Migrate

Flask-Migrate handles database migrations with SQLAlchemy.

- **Installation:**

```bash
pip install Flask-Migrate
```

- **Configuration:**
```

```python
from flask_migrate import Migrate

migrate = Migrate(app, db)
```

- **Usage:**

```bash
flask db init
flask db migrate -m "Initial migration."
flask db upgrade
```

2.3 Creating Your Own Extension

Creating your own extension allows for

modular reuse and sharing of code. Here's a step-by-step guide:

2.3.1 Basic Structure

- **Create the package structure:**

```
myextension/
├── myextension/
│   ├── __init__.py
│   └── core.py
├── tests/
└── setup.py
```

- **Define the extension in `__init__.py`:**

```python
class MyExtension:
    def __init__(self, app=None):
        if app is not None:
            self.init_app(app)

    def init_app(self, app):
        # Initialize the extension with the app
        pass
```

- **Create a `setup.py` file for distribution:**

```python
from setuptools import setup

setup(
    name='myextension',
```

```python
    version='0.1',

    packages=['myextension'],

    install_requires=[

        'Flask',

    ],

)
```

- **Install and use the extension:**

```bash
pip install .
```

```python
from flask import Flask

from myextension import MyExtension
```

```python
app = Flask(__name__)
my_ext = MyExtension(app)
```

3. Insights

3.1 Best Practices in Flask Development

- **Code Modularization:**

Structure your Flask project into modules to keep code clean and manageable. Use Blueprints to organize routes.

```python
from flask import Blueprint

main = Blueprint('main', __name__)

@main.route('/')
```

```python
def index():

    return "Hello, World!"
```

- **Configuration Management:**

Use separate configuration files for development and production environments.

```python
app.config.from_object('config.DevelopmentConfig')
```

- **Using Virtual Environments:**

Keep dependencies isolated by using virtual environments.

```bash
```

```
python3 -m venv venv

source venv/bin/activate

```
```

3.2 Performance Optimization

- **Profiling and Analysis:**

  Use profiling tools to identify performance
  bottlenecks.

  - **Flask-DebugToolbar** can help
  visualize queries and performance metrics.

- **Database Indexing:**

  Ensure that database tables are well-indexed
  to improve query speed.

- **Static File Caching:**

  Configure a CDN (Content Delivery
```

Network) to serve static files and reduce server load.

3.3 Security in Flask Applications

- **CSRF Protection:**

  Use extensions like Flask-WTF to protect your forms from CSRF vulnerabilities.

- **Input Sanitization:**

  Clean and validate all user input to prevent XSS and SQL Injection attacks.

- **Credential Management:**

  Avoid storing credentials in source code. Use environment variables and credential management services.

Deploying a Flask app, using extensions, and following best practices are fundamental to ensuring the success of your web applications. Preparation for production, Docker usage, and choosing the right extensions can significantly improve your app's quality and scalability. Similarly, maintaining high standards of security and performance is essential to providing an optimal user experience and protecting user data. By adhering to these guidelines, you can develop and manage robust and reliable Flask applications.

Index